REACHING OUT
TO
RIGHT RELATIONSHIPS

Stanislaus Kennedy RSC

VERITAS

First Published 1998 by
Veritas Publications
7-8 Lower Abbey Street
Dublin 1

Copyright © Stanislaus Kennedy RSC 1998

ISBN 1 85390 333 7

The author and publishers are grateful for permission to reproduce copyright material:
'Saint Francis and the Sow', from *Three Books*. Copyright© 1993 by Galway Kinnell. Previously published in *Mortal Acts, Mortal Words* (1980). Reprinted by Houghton Mifflin Co. All rights reserved. Extract from *Conjectures of a Guilty Bystander*, by Thomas Merton, by permission of Burns & Oates; extract from *Selected Poems of Ranier Maria Rilke: A translation from German and Commentary* by Robert Blyth© 1981 HarperCollins.

British Library Cataloguing
in Publication Data.
A catalogue record for
this book is available
from the British Library.

Photographs: Vincent Dixon
Cover design by Barbara Croatto
Printed in the Republic of Ireland by Paceprint Ltd, Dublin

Contents

Introduction 5

Right relationships with ourselves 13

Right relationships with others 19

Right relationships with the world and society 31

Right relationships with the environment 37

Right relationships with God 43

Conclusion 47

Acknowledgment

I wish to thank all the people who made this booklet possible, especially Vincent Dixon, for the beautiful photographs which he produced so generously. I would also like to thank most sincerely: Úna O'Connor, Jennifer Holland, Bernice Turner and Síle Wall who all contributed to the typing. A very special thanks to Siobhán Parkinson for her wonderful assistance with the editing. And, finally, to the publishers, Veritas, who have been so courteous and generous at all times.

Monday, 16 February 1998

Introduction

Our relationships

In order to live our lives to the best, we need to have right relationships, with ourselves, with others, with society, with the environment and with God. Our humanity is inextricably linked with everything in the universe. As Dylan Thomas expresses it: 'The force that through the green fuse drives the flower drives my green age... The force that drives the water through the rocks drives my red blood.' Thomas Merton puts it like this: 'Sipping a cup of green tea, I stopped the war.'

This book invites us to explore the beauty within us and around us and the possibilities and potential of the transforming power of God, of friends and relations, of the poor, of society, of nature and the earth, at work in each of us if we are attentive to it. It is about relationships and the intimate interplay between our relationship with ourselves (who we are and how we relate to who we are), our relationships with the people around us (how we relate to our families, colleagues at work and out of work), our relationship with society (how we relate to and perceive society, its structures and instruments – political, economic and social), our relationship with the earth (our concern for our environment), and our relationship with God (how we relate to our God, the God of our hearts, the God of our lives). This book invites us to explore the interplay of love between God, the universe and our own hearts. It invites us to a self-acceptance that enables us to take on and

Right Relationships

understand a whole new family of friends and relations and to let go of preconceived perceptions and preoccupations and ideas.

Hands
The text is interspersed with photographs of hands, which are intended to express different relationships. I have used hands as an expression of different types of relationships. The uniqueness of my hands reminds me of my own uniqueness, my preciousness in God's sight. In the hand I see the gentleness with which I can touch. The ordinariness of hands reveals to me that my own spiritual growth takes place in the ordinary events of everyday life. The hand represents for me a very strong image of life, its emptiness and its fullness, its flaws and its blessings. In the hand I see my openness to others, or lack of it, and their openness, or lack of it, to me. I see my readiness or my lack of readiness to see and to hear what society is saying and teaching me, and what I can bring to it. In the hand I see the reaching out for forgiveness and reconciliation. I have learned that the hand is my opportunity to reach out to other people, to the world, to the universe and to God and to be held by them. In the hand I see my emptiness and my thirst for relationships. In the hand I also see the wonderful gift of being able to touch and experience all that the universe contains and sends me.

The hands represent life, a gift that is meant to be given and shared as a generous expression of love. My life must be one of gratitude for all those people, events, moments and situations which have touched, changed, gifted and transformed my life.

Using this book as a prayer guide
I hope that this book, which centres on the many facets of relationships, will inspire you to grow in your relationships with yourself, with other people and with God, and that the

Our Relationships

photographs will assist you to reflect more deeply on these relationships. There is no right or best way to use this booklet: that depends on you and your needs. In case you wish to use the book as a guide for prayer, I have included some reflections at the end of each chapter, which you may find useful, and which you can adapt in a way that is fitting for you.

Some helpful ideas on prayer practice

It is vital that we all pray and reflect in the way that is best for us, but here are some ideas that may help. First, I think it is important to choose a space and time for prayer each day. It may be difficult to find a space in a hectic life or a hectic home where we can have solitude, but it is important to search for it, find it and then hold on to it. The space may be a corner of the bedroom or garden, somewhere at the office or on a bus or train. It doesn't matter where it is, as long as it is a place where you can be quiet and a place you can make sacred for yourself.

Finding the time may also be difficult. Try starting to carve ten minutes out of your day, preferably in the morning, and then expand it to twenty or thirty minutes if you can. This means making choices about not spending that time on something else. Of course there will be days when you genuinely won't have the time, but if that happens, just begin again the next day.

Our lives today are all about activities, noise, business, moving, coming and going. It is always a struggle to get started on prayer, but when you do start you will find that the struggle is worth it because you will notice a change in yourself, a deepening of your awareness of yourself and of others and of what is happening around you, and a deepening of your awareness of and desire for God.

I suggest that you begin each prayer practice by asking God to help you and acknowledging that it is God's work and not yours. I have included a breathing prayer in each practice (at the end of each section of the book). Breathing easily, regularly and attentively slows us down and calms our minds and bodies. A word or brief phrase is suggested when you are breathing in and another when you are breathing out. This practice can, with time, be a helpful way to clear the mind and heart and make it easier to enter inner life with God.

I suggest also that you use your hands to make a connection between your relationship with God and your daily life. It's also a good idea in each prayer practice to read a few verses of scripture, which may assist you in hearing what God is saying to you and what God is calling you to. Then, towards the end of each prayer time, I suggest that you give time to reflection, reflecting on what has happened during your prayer, the desires and the stirrings in your heart. And, finally, I suggest that at the end of each prayer practice you write down your experience in a journal you keep for the purpose. This way you can attain a greater consciousness of what happened during your time in prayer; recording it can help you to preserve your experience so that you can go back to it that evening again, when you look back on your day, giving thanks for it and seeing the connection between your day and your prayer practice. It can also help in reviewing your day and your week.

Right relationships with ourselves

To have a right relationship with ourselves, we need to be at one with ourselves. We need to have a sense that we are precious in God's sight, to realise that we are gift, that God has called us by name, that he loves us and that he has put us into this world to make a unique contribution. To have this deep realisation of preciousness is to have a love of life and a love of ourselves, and it is to be deeply tuned in to the giver of life and deeply grateful to that giver.

Remembering our own preciousness

Sometimes we need to be reminded of our own loveliness and our own preciousness. Perhaps this poem by Galway Kinnel will help to explain what I mean:

> **St Francis and the Sow**
> The bud
> stands for all things
> even for those things that don't flower,
> for everything flowers, from within, of self-blessing:
> though sometimes it is necessary
> to reteach a thing its loveliness,
> to put a hand on its brow
> of the flower
> and retell it in words and in touch
> it is lovely
> until it flowers again from within, of self-blessing:

> as Saint Francis
> put his hand on the creased forehead
> of the sow, and told her in words and in touch
> blessings of earth on the sow, and the sow
> began remembering all down her thick length,
> from the earthen snout all the way
> through the fodder and slops
> to the spiritual curl of the tail,
> from hard spininess spiked out from the spine
> down through the great broken heart
> to the blue milken dreaminess spurting and shuddering
> from the fourteen teats into the fourteen mouths
>   sucking and blowing beneath them:
> the long, perfect loveliness of the sow.

Do we feel that we are gift? Or do we just feel that we are doing a bit? Maybe we're not good enough, maybe we are not as good as we should be? And one day we hope that we will do a bit better, that we will be able to love ourselves a bit more. Unless we start loving ourselves now and realise our preciousness, we are wasting our lives. And in any case, by whose standards are we judging ourselves? Are we denying God's goodness? Are we denying and ungrateful towards the unique contribution that we, and only we, can make?

Inner peace

To have a right relationship with ourselves means to have an inner peace, which is also a gift from God. Jesus says to us: Peace is my farewell gift to you. I do not give it to you as the world gives it. The peace Jesus gives us is harmony, serenity – which includes dignity, composure and graciousness – silence, stillness and tranquillity – which implies a command of our emotions, an ability to remain unagitated even in the midst of danger or excitement.

It is no easy task to maintain peace as we go about

Right relationships with ourselves

building a more just and non-violent world. Often many issues and causes are competing for our attention, many organisations want us to join them, there are many books and reports and newspapers that we feel we need to read. If we are to find ways to nurture the peace we already have and to render ourselves open to receive this essential gift of peace, we need to take time off for rest and play and prayer.

We need to ask ourselves questions: Where do I find rest? Why do I find it difficult to take time off? Is it because I can't face my limitations? Am I afraid that I am not able to do as much work as I would like to do effectively, or as much work as someone whom I greatly admire?

Sometimes we may be overwhelmed by a sense of duty and feelings of responsibility that trap us into overworking. Many of us have inherited the work ethic, which leads us sometimes to feel the need to prove ourselves loveable by working. The more we do, the more loveable we think we are. But that is an endless spiral that ends in exhaustion and it is a form of violence against ourselves.

It doesn't stop with ourselves, either, because if we overdo things and over-stretch ourselves, it can be very unpleasant to be around us. If we overwork for the wrong reasons, it is not good for those we are working with, and that is a form of violence against them. St Paul said, 'The willingness to give should accord with one's means to give, not go beyond them. The relief of others ought not to impoverish you' *(2 Corinthians 8:12)*. One way to understand those words of St Paul is that working to secure the rights of others, helping to restore or enhance the dignity of others should not result in our becoming dehumanised ourselves; helping others to be less dehumanised should not dehumanise us.

Daily prayer practice

1: Prayer
Place yourself in God's presence.

2: Reading
Read a passage from 'Right relationships with ourselves'.

3: Breathing prayer
Breathing in: I am [insert your name]
Breathing out: Thank you, God

4: Scripture
For it was you who formed my inward parts
You knit me together in my mother's womb
I praise you for I am wonderfully made
Wonderful are your works
(Psalm 139:13-14)

5: Hands
Notice your hands, their colour, shape and size. How have they served you? Notice their flaws and imperfections. Notice what is beautiful about them. Picture yourself in God's hands. Imagine God smiling and enjoying who you are and hear God say: I formed you, I called you by name, you are precious in my sight and I love you.

6: Journal
Write down your experience of God smiling and enjoying who you are and calling you by your name.

7: Prayer
Ask God to remind you often during the day that you are wonderfully made.

RIGHT RELATIONSHIPS WITH OTHERS

Having a right relationship with others means being able to have a right relationship with ourselves. It means being able to recognise our preciousness but it also means being able to recognise our own weaknesses, the shadow side of ourselves, leading us to treat others with compassion. But often we don't do this. We allow conflict and tension to dominate our relationships with others. What is happening out there in the world – war and civil strife – can happen in our personal relationships too. We can play win/lose games with our colleagues and associates just as easily as the super-powers do. We can hurl missiles at people with whom we don't agree. These things happen in our misunderstandings, our failure to communicate, our resentment, prejudice, avoidance of others, our silent treatment of others, our self-righteousness, our impatience with others, our desire for power over others. It happens in communities, with co-workers, with neighbours and with friends. The seeds of injustice and violence exist within each person.

Jesus identifies himself with the poor
It is by standing back from these conflicts and following the example of Jesus that we can develop right relationships with others: 'I assure you as often as you did it unto one of these, you did it unto me' *(Matthew 25: 40)*, Jesus tells us. Here he identifies himself with the hungry, those who are

thirsty, the stranger, those who are ill, those who languish in prison. At the conversion of St Paul in the Acts of the Apostles, Jesus discloses a further identification with those who are afflicted or in any way persecuted. When Saul was on the road to Damascus, the voice that spoke to him identified himself thus: 'I am Jesus, the one you are persecuting.' We should ask ourselves *'Who would Jesus say that about today?'*

Jesus makes the insignificant significant

The woman at the well to whom Jesus spoke was the most outcast person. She was the wrong race, the wrong sex, the wrong religion and in the wrong place at the wrong time, and yet she was the first person to whom Jesus revealed his divinity. A prostitute was the first person whom he told that he was the Son of God. The incident of the woman taken in adultery who was about to be stoned by the people is similar. Jesus revealed their injustice to those who were about to cast stones and made the person who was identified as a sinner significant.

The story Jesus told about the man in charge of the vineyard who hired people at different hours of the day and at the end of the day paid them all the same is a parable about making the insignificant significant. The people who weren't selected in the morning were the insignificant ones. They were weak, feeble people – rejects. In that story, Jesus turned the values of his day and our day upside down. He made those feeble people as significant as the people who were able to do a full day's work.

Walking with the poor

Jesus walked with the poor, and by walking with the poor, he gave us an example of what we can all do. But it is not easy to walk with the poor, the marginalised, the disabled, the elderly, those with special needs. It is easier to do 'good work' for the poor. A person could work in a soup kitchen all her or his life, work with the poor, and still never walk with them. Walking with the poor means recognising that no matter how poor or deprived people may be, they carry within them the great beauty of God. Do we allow them to reveal that beauty to us? We can serve the poor and not love them, but we cannot walk with them without loving them. Loving and walking is the form that justice and caring must take.

We know the story of the Good Samaritan, and of the two people who passed by and did not help the man who had been attacked. We must ask ourselves: Why did they pass by, and why did the Samaritan stop? I think the reason may be that they asked themselves different questions. The priest and the Levite may have asked, What will happen to me if I stop and become involved with this man? I could be beaten. I could be robbed. The question asked by the Samaritan, on the other hand, was something more like this: What will happen to *him* if I don't stop, if I don't walk with him? Asking the right questions is more important than finding the right answers.

Loving our enemies

Having right relationships with others must include right relationships with those who have hurt us, the enemy. Having right relationships with the enemy demands that we face ourselves and each other with honesty and awareness. It challenges us to free ourselves from old habits and blind spots, and develop the full range of our powers, sensitivities and depth as human beings. We can struggle to hold on to the old ways, or we can learn to use the difficulties in our relationships as opportunities to awaken and bring forth our finest human qualities, such as awareness, compassion, humour, wisdom and a fearless dedication to truth. If we choose this approach, even the most difficult relationships become a path that can deepen our connection with ourselves and with those we love with great difficulty as well as those we love easily. The poet Rainer Maria Rilke put it this way:

> The man who cannot quietly close his eyes
> Certain that there is vision after vision
> Inside, simply waiting until night-time
> To rise all around him in the darkness.
> It's all over for him, he's like an old man.

Loving the enemy – a challenge and a cost

Learning to love our enemy challenges us, because it often costs us what we hold most dear, namely our old ways of staying secure and defended. There is a promise in such a situation that is equally powerful – if we open up in the ways it requires, our relationships will deepen immeasurably and we will broaden out as human beings, becoming more flexible, loving, responsive to life as a whole. Every relationship carries moments of pain, when we cannot get what we want, or cannot resolve our differences, when we rub up against hurtful, ugly or constricted places in ourselves or the areas that we cannot stand. In truth we all have certain tendencies which cause even our best friends to find us hard to be with. No matter how delightful or highly developed they may be, two individuals will never fit together perfectly. Even in the best of relationships there will always be rough edges and problems that can't be entirely resolved, because we are creatures of this earth, with all the limitations and imperfections that entails. Human relationships cannot always manifest the perfect, unconditional love we know and feel in our hearts.

Heartbreak

When we feel the pain of this constriction between the perfect love in our hearts and the obstacles to its complete realisation in earthly form, it breaks our heart. This is not a bad thing. When the heart breaks open we hurt, and in this pain is our basic openness to life. When we feel raw and tender, we are in touch with the very core of who we are. The heart can never really break, though, for it is already by nature soft and receptive. When our heart breaks, what really breaks is the defensive shell which we have constructed to try to protect our soft spot, where we feel most deeply affected by life. When that is exposed, we feel the vivid presence of reality as never before. Sooner or later, we inevitably discover that the world we love cannot give us everything, or be everything we would like, or understand us perfectly. Nor can we ourselves be the ideal person. But what we can always do whenever we encounter the imperfections in ourselves or in those we love, is to break open our heart, let it keep expanding, until it can embrace the painful reality that we are facing.

When our heart breaks out of the protective shell we have built around it, and we shed our ideal images of how a relationship should be, we may feel naked. It is in this nakedness that we taste the essential nature of our existence. The truth is that we have no ultimate control over what happens to us in this life; therefore to feel naked and vulnerable is to be in direct contact with reality.

People who are not for us

There are always people with whom we don't agree, who block us, who contradict us, who stifle us, people who are not 'for us'. Their presence seems to bring out in us either aggression or a sort of regression; others bring out envy and jealousy – they are everything we wish we were ourselves, and their presence reminds us that we are not. They ask too much of us, we can't respond to their demands, so we push them away. These are the enemies who endanger us, and even if we dared to admit it, we are afraid of them. We dislike them, we might even hate them – not in a deep, mortal sense, not even deliberately, but

Right Relationships

nevertheless we wish these people didn't exist. These feelings between different personalities are natural – they come from our own background, our childhood, and our emotional immaturity. But if we let ourselves be guided by them, then we will become more and more shut in on ourselves, blocked off from others. Our enemies frighten us. We are incapable of hearing their cries and responding to their needs. Their aggression or domination stifles us, we flee from them or wish that they would disappear. They highlight for us our own weakness, our lack of maturity, our inner poverty, and this is difficult to look at. The faults we see in them are often the ones we refuse to face in ourselves.

Forgiveness and reconciliation
The message of Jesus is clear: 'I say to you here, love your enemies; do good to those who hate you; bless those who curse you; pray for those who abuse you; to him who strikes you on the cheek, offer the other also. If you love those who love you, what credit is that to you? For even sinners love those who love them' *(Luke 6:27; 9:32)*. Christ's own life demonstrated for us the power of love. Christ came not to judge us, not to condemn us, but to heal, to save, to guide us on the path of love; to forgive us because he loves us to the depth of our being, and that was his one request to us, that we love as he had loved, as he had loved his enemies and his friends.

Therein lies our hope. It is possible to accept ourselves and our darkness and our weakness and our flaws and our fears, because of God's love. We are not imprisoned forever by egoism and darkness; it is possible to love and so it becomes possible to accept others and to forgive. As long as we see in the other only those qualities that reflect our own, no growth is possible. The relationship remains static and, sooner or later, it will end or flare up. A relationship is only authentic and stable when it is founded on the

Right relationships with others

acceptance of weakness and forgiveness and the hope of growth. This is the heart of reconciliation – the heart of forgiveness. We will always need forgiveness, and always need to be forgiving and forgiven, because in spite of all the trust we may have in each other, there will always be words that wound, attitudes that hurt, situations that cause pain, expectations that are not met, and that is the cross that is part of our daily lives. The cross means a constant effort, daily acceptance and mutual forgiveness. St Paul says,

> Put on then as God's chosen ones, holy and beloved, compassion, kindness, lowliness, meekness and patience, forbearing one another; and if one has a complaint against another, forgiving each other as the Lord has forgiven you, so you also must forgive. But above all these, put on love, which binds everything together in perfect harmony and let the peace of Christ rule in your hearts, to which indeed you were called in the one body; and be thankful. *(Colossians 3:12-15)*

Our vision of humanity

In all this, our vision of humanity is very important. We must recognise our common humanity, and the fact that we are all human beings, and we are weak and strong, rich and poor, important and unique; we are all precious in the sight of God. Because we are precious, we are not condemned to oppression or hatred, and each of us can allow the power of healing to bring balance into our lives. If we look at the wider world, we see not only the power of healing within people, we see men and women all over the world who give witness to love and peace and reconciliation; men and women who can help others to rediscover their source in the God of peace. These men and women are rooted in a vision of faith and the call of humanity to unity and they, through who they are or what they are or what they do, can help others to struggle for peace and reconciliation. This vision of humanity, this vision of faith and trust, this vision and conviction of the divine power hidden within each of us, can play a major role in the process of reconciliation with the enemy, the transformation of the person we despise into someone we respect and listen to.

Wishing the enemy well
We need also to be determined to make definite efforts to struggle not to be overcome by fear, depression or apathy. We begin by wishing the enemy well, recognising that he or she has a right to a place in the world, to be himself or herself, with his or her limitations and poverty, with his or her gifts. This acknowledgement implies a definite gesture – not speaking badly of them or putting them down, the struggle to forgive consistently, seeing, thinking and believing there are good things in everyone, and about everyone, and constantly trying to discover these good things. We need to understand the enemy in terms of their background or wounds, their particular fragility; we need to turn the judgement which leads to anger and hatred into understanding and compassion.

Accepting and respecting the enemy
The process of transforming the enemy into someone whom we respect and accept takes time, effort and discipline. It certainly comes from the hidden force of God, but it also comes from the thousands of efforts that we make daily to accept others just as they are, to forgive them, to accept ourselves also, with all our wounds and fragility, the enemies within us; it comes also from learning to cope with our own wounds, fears and anguish and from using them in a positive way. We should try never to turn away from the enemy or from conflict. When the time is right, we should try to confront them.

Right relationships with others

Outpouring of love

Forgiveness and reconciliation are about the outpouring of love. When we experience these moments in our lives, we experience a kind of conversion that opens us to new horizons. This conversion reveals certain truths about ourselves and helps us to see areas in our lives that we need to change. Parts of us are awakened, and we begin to discover in our lives resources we never dreamed we possessed. We discover our potential to love, to care, to forgive, to be compassionate, to heal. We are fragile vessels whose love often gets tired. We need to be converted over and over again, and so the healing act of our growth continues. We empty ourselves that we may be filled. We forgive that we may be forgiven. We heal and we are healed. We discover it is not so much what we do that touches lives as who we are, and who we are becoming. Painful though it may be, we discover the great truth for ourselves, that what is most important is not how much of ourselves we leave with others, but how much we enable others to be themselves. We give thanks to God and to those who have shown us our potential to be healers, reconcilers, and at the same time are healed and reconciled ourselves.

Forgiveness heals

'Finding himself cured, one of them turned back, praising God at the top of his voice.' This is the story of the leper who gave thanks, from Luke 17:15. There are moments when healing takes place in our lives, and the only way we can explain the healing is by living it, and in no place is that more true than in reconciliation. When we are reconciled with another, healing has taken place within ourselves. Like the awakened leper, we turn back, praising God at the top of our voice, because we can't help it, because in reaching out to others, we have been transformed ourselves.

Daily prayer practice

1: Prayer
Place yourself in God's presence.

2: Reading
Read a passage from 'Right relationships with others'.

3: Breathing prayer
Breathing in: Divine compassion
Breathing out: Teach me

4: Scripture
When I was hungry you gave me food
When I was thirsty you gave me to drink
When I was naked you gave me clothing
When I was a stranger you welcomed me
When I was sick you took care of me
When I was in prison you visited me
(Matthew 25:31-45)

5: Hands
Remember compassionate people you have known. Remember their hands. How did they use their hands to show mercy? Try to remember how they used them to express forgiveness. Picture yourself in the company of Jesus and experience his giving, compassionate, merciful, forgiving hands.

6: Journal
Write down the key things you have learned about compassion for other people and about God's compassion.

7: Prayer
Ask God to revive and renew the gift of compassion in you this day.

RIGHT RELATIONSHIPS WITH THE WORLD AND SOCIETY

The third area where we need to have right relationships is in relation to society and the world. We need to have right relationships with the human environments, the social structures, institutions and processes, for example business corporations, government, the media, the churches, the law. People's dignity is greatly affected by structures which can serve either to build up a person's dignity or to hinder the growth of individuals or whole groups of people. It is important here to reflect on the fact that it is the dignity of the human person that makes economic and political issues moral issues.

Standing back from consumerism

Part of having a right relationship with the world is standing back from the consumerism that has such a hold on us. Our society has drifted into a pattern of constant consumption, and consumption has become a powerful dynamic, keeping us from a more holistic way of life. Once considered a chore, shopping has now become for some people a passion and a pastime. Consumerism is mainly an affliction of the affluent, but the poor are also captivated by the dream, fed by sleek and subtle television commercials, of living better through acquiring more and better possessions.

The belief that more is better pressurises us to work harder and longer just to make ends meet. As the cost of living increases, so do our work hours – for those of us who have work. The tendency to consume more than we need is fuelled by advertisers whose livelihoods depend on creating expanding needs. Advertisers aim to convince us that what we have is not enough and that happiness is just one more purchase away. Manufacturers too fuel our discontent with the strategy of planned obsolescence. Consumerism's hold on us relies on the hopes and the expectations we place on consumer products. We buy brand names and designer labels in the hope that they will increase our self-esteem and raise our social status. The latest fashions promise to make us attractive and appealing, thus playing to our unmet need to be loved. Advertisers promise that their products will fill the voids in our lives, fulfilling not only our physical needs but also our emotional longings.

These subliminal messages are so effective that people concentrate on owning a house and filling it with furnishings, when what they really crave is the emotional construct of home. In a consumer society, material goods are called upon to serve as reassurance of love and care, as when absent parents attempt to assuage their children's feelings of abandonment and their own guilt by indulging them with every imaginable toy or game.

The example of great people
But of course we can't buy self-esteem or affection or admiration or love with money or with consumer goods. We will only come to have a right relationship with society by following the example of those great people who have fought for justice and peace in the world: people like Dorothy Day, who gave her whole life to working for the poor and the homeless and at the same time actively campaigned for an end to war and to the arms race; people like Martin Luther King, who was on fire for justice, and believed that the pursuit of violence at any time was morally wrong. King saw that not only was the war in

Right relationships with the world and society

Vietnam wrong in itself, but it also worked to drain resources away from programmes for his own people. This made him aware that 'America would never invest the necessary funds of energies in rehabilitation of its poor so long as adventures like Vietnam continued to draw men, skills and money like some demoniac destructive suction tube. So I was increasingly compelled to see the war as an enemy of the poor and to attack it as such.' And not only did the war draw resources away from the poor, it also took the sons of the poor and sent them to a foreign country to uphold rights and liberties that they themselves were denied at home.

Caring within community

We are constantly bombarded by news coverage of hardships and tragedies in the world, and this can so overwhelm us that we feel it is too much for us to deal with. One way to learn to deal with problems of society is to learn to care within a community. Community is the reality that makes it possible for us to see the huge pain in our world and still be moved by compassion to do something about it. With the support of a community, we can witness the pain of the human family without turning away or becoming angered by our impotence, because in community we experience the strength and the power that comes from pooling our resources.

True abundance arises from the simple experience of people being present to one another and for one another. Caring within a community requires that we trade our individualistic and competitive attitudes for attitudes that appreciate and encourage the unique gifts each member brings to the group. Community allows us to benefit from the diverse gifts and charisms of the different members of the group and allows us to reach out to others with compassion.

Daily prayer practice

1: Prayer
Place yourself in God's presence.

2: Reading
Read a passage from 'Right relationships with the world and society'.

3: Breathing prayer
Breathing in: We are many
Breathing out: We are one

4: Scripture
For just as the body is one and has many members and all the members of the body, though many, are one body, so it is with Christ... Now you are the body of Christ.
(1 Corinthians 12:12, 31)

5: Hands
Imagine your hands joined and connected with all the hands around the world, forming one circle of loving trust. Be open to give what is being asked of you and to receive what is being given to you.

6: Journal
Write down your experience of being part of the body of Christ.

7: Prayer
Ask God to make you more aware of your connectedness with the whole of humanity.

RIGHT RELATIONSHIPS WITH THE ENVIRONMENT

The world in which we live and work is very complex and very fragile. Today we are reminded again and again about the complexity and fragility of the earth. Advances in science and technology have brought with them a host of serious new problems, and unexpected catastrophes. Throughout history we have had good reason to fear for the very future of the earth. In the past our fear had to do with nuclear weapons; now we need to be capable of appreciating the signs of impending ecological disaster.

Reckless abuse of the environment
We must think about the enormous quantities of pollutants emitted into the air every day, by our factories, cars and domestic dwellings. Nuclear accidents, industrial heat and pollution of lakes and rivers have resulted in the loss of millions of square miles of forests, together with hundreds of indigenous species. The reckless use and thoughtless abuse of animals, toxic waste, mountains of virtually indestructible garbage, global warming and the depletion of the ozone layer are not new, but for decades we have been unaware of them, or the voices of those who were aware of them fell on deaf ears. No doubt there are many reasons for this, among them failure to provide basic scientific information to most of the general public; lack of agreement on the possible causes of ecological problems among scientists; powerful business interests which hide or

minimise obvious or blatant harm which is being done to the environment. Perhaps people simply feel that nature can take care of itself.

In addition to these things, and in a way far more significant, is the fact that many of us are not confronted directly and immediately with the problems or their magnitude or consequences. We are simply unaware of the price to be paid eventually by our people and places in sustaining our type of lifestyle, the one we are accustomed to. We tend to think naively about the resources at our disposal. They seem limitless. Yet we know the opposite is true. We perceive the poor and the underdeveloped countries naively, we wish that all people could enjoy a good standard of living, we have no comprehension of what the consequences would be in terms of energy consumption, natural resource depletion, pollution and waste generation.

Reverence for nature

There is another reason too that we do not pay attention to the voices that remind us of what is happening. It is because we do not pay attention to nature. We do not revere it, we treat it as an object. We can delight in its beauty, but for the most part it serves simply as the stage for our exploits and raw materials for our designs. As Christians we face a real challenge — to bring about a conversion in attitudes and behaviour in relation to the earth and all beings on the earth. The challenge is to empower and support those men and women who work for ecologically sound policies and practices. The challenge is to believe that in doing that we are actually carrying out our responsibilities as Christians, Christians who see the world as God's creation, because this is the result of the free and loving action of God. In Psalm 19 we read,

> The heavens are telling the glory of God; they are a marvellous display of God's craftsmanship. Day and

Right relationships with the environment

night they keep on telling about God. Without a sound or a word, silent in the skies, their message reaches out to all the world. *(Psalm 19:1-4)*

For the believer, no creature is too humble or insignificant to make God's presence known, for the very reality and existence of each is grounded in the mystery of God's desire to create a world of love and light. To the extent that our imagination is inspired and formed by the biblical vision of creation as a revelation of God's glory, our basic attitudes towards nature can be transformed.

When God created the earth, he saw that it was good. Thus creation is goodness. It is our obligation as Christians to emphasise the goodness of creation, not to be blind to the fact that much of what we experience in the world ought not to be. If our imagination is inspired by faith and hope we can look afresh at the world and see it has something good despite the powers of destruction and oppression which permeate it. The goodness and ultimate value of creation is determined by what divine love can do with it and intends for it. Thus Christians affirm that good creation comprises the entire history of God's relation to the world from its beginning to the end. What we look for is a new attitude towards nature, one that is based on biblical vision, that is, the intrinsic relationship between humanity and the rest of the cosmos as the one creation of God.

The cosmos as creation

Our Christian tradition has something vitally important to offer us in the face of the ecological crisis, because we recognise that the natural world is of eternal significance as part of the whole cosmos of God's creation. It is this vision of the cosmos as God's creation, and not as humanity's warehouse or playground, that can challenge the individualism, utilitarianism and greed that plague the

Right Relationships

modern attitude towards nature, especially in the western world. It is our vision as Christians of the human race that people are created in God's image and carry responsibility as co-creators with God for creation.

One of the greatest tasks facing us today is to transform our own relationship and the relationship of others with the cosmos, with the earth. It cannot be left to a few professionals to create a new consciousness and new attitudes towards nature. It is up to us to inspire this new vision.

Daily prayer practice

1: Prayer
Place yourself in God's presence.

2: Reading
Read a passage from 'Right relationships with the environment'.

3: Breathing prayer
Breathing in: I am alive
Breathing out: I am aware

4: Scripture
What return shall I make to God
For all God's bounty to me?
I will lift up the cup of salvation
And call on the name of God
(Psalm 116:12-19)

5: Hands
Imagine you are blind and your hands are touching the earth, the flowers, the rain, the rock formations. Be aware of what it feels like to touch into the goodness of God expressed in the universe.

6: Journal
Write down something for which you are grateful, which has come to your awareness during this prayer and for which you rarely give thanks.

7: Prayer
Give thanks for God's steadfast love.

RIGHT RELATIONSHIPS WITH GOD

Having right relationships with ourselves, with others around us and with our society and the environment brings us into a right relationship with God. To sustain those relationships, and to sustain our relationship with God we need to be reflective, we need to have a sense of prayer and contemplation.

Prayer and contemplation
That sense of prayer and contemplation is what is missing for many of us in our lives today. We are so busy working, doing overtime, holding down two or even more jobs, that we are losing our prayer time, our time to stop and rest and evaluate what we are doing with our working time and what it is for. Of course we need to work, and of course we are under pressure to work harder and harder in the modern world. Working mothers are particularly under pressure, holding down a job during the day and still carrying the major responsibility at home for housework and children. But a lot of that pressure comes from our grasping consumerism, our longing to buy and to own, in order to have self-esteem and to make ourselves lovable and attractive. We feel the need to work continuously to earn the money to buy the things that we believe are going to make us happy.

A sense of Sabbath
None of us should be so busy that we don't have time for prayer, time to reflect, time to be able to distinguish

between the urgent and the important. In Genesis we read about God creating a day of rest, the Sabbath. The rabbis insisted that the Sabbath was vital to creation because it equalised the rich and the poor, because for at least one day the rich and the poor were equally free from the constraints of work. Secondly, it was an opportunity and a time to evaluate the week's work, as God evaluated the work of creation, to determine whether what they were doing was good. And, thirdly, observation of the Sabbath was meant to give us time to contemplate the meaning of life, which, of course, is critically important.

For these same reasons, observing the Sabbath is equally important today, especially in light of the dangers of overwork. On the Sabbath a different spirit holds sway than on other days of the week. There is a different climate and mood. The rabbis said that as the Jew enters into the Sabbath, so the Sabbath enters into the Jew; it was not so much that the Jew kept the Sabbath as that the Sabbath kept the Jew. Perhaps even more than our predecessors on this planet we badly need the Sabbath, but the Sabbath is more richly understood as an atmosphere rather than as a date.

If we think of Sabbath not so much as a particular day of the week, but as a commitment to time for prayer, reflection and solitude, we can begin to understand what Thomas Merton describes in his book, *The Conjectures of a Guilty Bystander*:

> At the centre of our being is a point of nothingness which is untouched by sin and by illusion, a point of pure truth, a point or spark which belongs entirely to God, which is never at our disposal, from which God disposes of our lives, which is inaccessible to the fantasies of our own mind or the brutalities of our own will. This little point of nothingness and of *absolute poverty* is the pure glory of God in us. It is so

to speak His name written in us, as our poverty, as our indigence, as our dependence, as our sonship. It is like a pure diamond, blazing with the invisible light of heaven. It is in everybody, and if we could see it we would see these billions of points of light coming together in the face and blaze of a sun that would make all the darkness and cruelty of life vanish completely.

In order to be able to appreciate what Merton is talking about, we all need to have a quiet space where we live or work. It may be our room, it may be a special place within our place of work, where we can simply be alone, in solitude, with ourselves and our God.

The temptation to lose ourselves in busyness and in things is strong, in order, perhaps, to buttress a shaky self-esteem or to escape lonely and painful reality and seek happiness in the glow that comes from the spending spree or the adrenaline high that is stoked by fast-paced action. But all of this prevents us from caring enough for ourselves and allowing the creative and caring side of ourselves to grow strong. When I talk about a sacred place or time, I am really talking about something that has a richness, that has an atmosphere; a place where we can enter more deeply into the true meaning of life, of relationships with ourselves, with each other as brothers and sisters and with the universe, with our God; above all, a place where we can experience the very deep sense, the beauty and preciousness of all creation.

Daily prayer practice

1: Prayer
Place yourself in God's presence.

2: Reading
Read a passage from 'Right relationships with God'.

3: Breathing prayer
Breathing in: You in me
Breathing out: I in you

4: Scripture
Open your mouth wide and I will fill it
I would feed you with the finest of wheat
And with honey from the rock I would satisfy you
(Psalm 81:10, 16)

5: Hands
Imagine your hands being clasped by somebody who loves you unconditionally. Receive and enjoy that unconditional love of God waiting to be poured out on you.

6: Journal
Write down your experience during this practice of God's unconditional love.

7: Prayer
Ask God to remove any obstacles that keep you from receiving his love.

Conclusion

To live our lives to the full and reach our full potential as human beings demands that we have right relationships. We all have a tendency to develop our relationships only partially, but if we have the right perspective we will be able to live our relationships to the full, discovering the vast possibilities that are in ourselves, in others and in the world.